Contents

INTRODUCTION

Electrical Wiring is a process of connecting cables and wires to the related devices such as fuse, switches, sockets, lights, fans etc to the main distribution board is a specific structure to the utility pole for continues power supply.

Wiring (a process of connecting various accessories for distribution of electrical energy from supplier's meter board to home appliances such as lamps, fans and other domestic appliances is known as Electrical Wiring) can be done using two methods which are: Joint box system or Tee system, Loop – in system.

An electrical box is a plastic or metal box used to connect wires and install devices such as switches, receptacles (outlets), and fixtures. An electrical box is almost always required for mounting devices and for housing wiring splices. Boxes come in many different sizes and several different shapes. A box must be sized appropriately for the number and size of wires entering the box. Metal electrical boxes must be grounded to the home's grounding system;

plastic boxes do not need grounding because they are nonconductive.

Each electrical circuit contains at least one "hot" wire that carries the electrical current from the service panel to the circuit devices and a neutral wire that carries current back to the service panel. Hot wires typically are black or red but can be other colors. Neutral wires typically are white. In some circuits, the neutral wire is used as a hot wire and the circuit has no dedicated neutral.

An electrical ground is a safety system that provides a safe path for electricity to follow in the event of a short circuit, electrical surge, or other safety or fire hazard. In modern home wiring systems, each circuit has its own ground wire that leads back to the service panel. After the panel, the ground system terminates at a ground rod driven into soil or to another ground conductor where electricity is safely dissipated into the earth. Older homes may have ground systems that rely on metal electrical boxes, metal conduit (which houses wiring), and metal water pipes.

CHAPTER ONE

A Brief History of Home Electrical Wiring

Electrical service to American homes began in the late 1890s and blossomed from 1920 to 1935, by which time 70 percent of American homes were connected to the electrical utility grid. In the following 200 some years, the methods for installing wiring in those homes has seen several important innovations aimed at improving the safety of electrical systems.

Knob-And-Tube Wiring

Between 1890 and 1910, a wiring system known as knob-and-tube was the principal system of installation. It was quite a dependable system for the time, and a surprising number of American homes still have knob-and-tube wiring functioning, where it is often found alongside more modern updates.

In knob-and-tube wiring, individually conducting wires protected by rubberized cloth fabric are installed in stud and joist cavities, held in place by porcelain knob insulators attached to the sides of framing members, and protected by porcelain tube insulators where the wires run through framing members. In this wiring system, hot wires and neutral wires were run separately for safety. The system also allowed long circuit runs to be constructed by splicing together lengths of wire. To do this, the insulation was stripped back, a new wire was wrapped around the exposed bare wire, and the splice was soldered together then taped to cover the splice. The downfall was the wire was exposed and there was no ground wire used.

Where knob-and-tube wiring is still functioning, it is living on borrowed time, since the rubberized cloth insulation used on the wires has an expected lifespan of about 25 years before it begins to crack and break down. Electrical systems containing functioning knob-and-tube wiring are in critical need of an upgrade. But just because you see knob-and-tubes in some wall or floor cavities, doesn't necessarily mean you are in danger. It was common practice to simply leave old wiring in place when a home was rewired. It's possible that the porcelain insulators and wires you see are merely antique remnants of earlier wiring installation. An electrician can tell you for sure.

Flexible Armored Cable (Greenfield)

In the 1920s to 1940s, electrical installations took a turn to a more protective wiring scheme—flexible armored cable. Flex, also known as Greenfield, was a welcomed addition to home wiring because the flexible metal walls helped to protect the wires from damage, and also offered a metal pathway that could ground the system when properly installed. Although it was an improvement, this wiring method had its troubles. Although the individual wire conductors are protected, the flexible outer metal jacket serves as a proper ground only when the metal pathway is complete all the way to the service entrance and grounding rod. There is still no separate ground wire in these installations.

First-Generation Sheathed Cable

In the 1930s, a quicker installation method was developed. Nonmetallic-sheathed cable was born, which incorporated a rubberized fabric coating sheath, much like knob and tube wiring, but here the hot and neutral wire were run together in this one sheathing. It also had its drawbacks due to the lack of a ground wire, but its development would eventually lead to major innovation. Early sheathed cable, however, also has an expected lifespan of about 25 years, and where it is still in use, such installations need to be upgraded.

Metal Conduit

The 1940s brought the age of metal conduit. This invention allowed users to pull many individual conducting wires in the same rigid metal tube enclosure. The conduit itself is considered a viable grounding method, and the system can also allow another separate grounding wire (usually an insulated green wire) to be pulled through the conduit. Conduit has been in use ever since those days and is still the recommended method for wiring in certain applications, such as when wiring needs to be run along the face of basement masonry walls or in exposed locations. Most homes have some areas where conduit is used, though it is now sometimes made with rigid plastic PVC conduit rather than metal.

Modern NM Cable

The newest addition to wiring was introduced in around 1965. The form of NM cable was an update to older NM cable, incorporating the use of a bare copper grounding wire that joined the insulated hot and neutral wires contained within the sheathing. Instead of rubberized sheathing, modern NM cable uses a very tough and durable vinyl sheathing. This update made the MN cable inexpensive and very easy to install. It is a very flexible product and is used extensively in virtually every new home built.

Along with NM cable for interior use, a related type of cable was also developed for underground use. Underground feeder wire (UF) can be buried directly under the ground without the need for a protecting conduit. This type of wire has a hot, a neutral, and a ground wire embedded in a solid plastic vinyl sheath that protects it from moisture. This offers an inexpensive method for running power underground to outbuildings and yard lights.

Metals Used in Wires

Through most of the history of residential electrical service, the preferred metal used in the conducting wires has been copper, known as the best conductor of electrical current. In the mid-1960s, when copper prices were quite high, aluminum came into vogue as a material for electrical wiring. Residential installations between 1965 and 1974 sometimes used wires that were solid aluminum, or aluminum covered with a thin layer of copper. Aluminum (AU) or copper-coated aluminum (AL-CU) wiring is perfectly safe if connected to receptacles, switches, and other devices rated for use with aluminum, but it can pose problems when it's installed with devices intended for use with copper wiring only. Because of these issues, aluminum or copper-clad aluminum is no longer used in residential applications. If you have aluminum wiring, repairs are best made by a professional.

Copper wire conductors in NM sheathed cable or in rigid metal or PVC plastic conduit has been the norm since the mid-1970s, and there are currently no new innovations in the wiring materials themselves. Recent safety improvements have involved the extended application of GFCI (ground-fault circuit interrupter) devices, and more recently, AFCI (arc-fault circuit interrupter) devices that help protect against fire and shock by sensing changes in current flow and shutting off power before problems occur. But the history of residential wiring is one of the periodic innovations that can revolutionize the industry. It is possible that another such innovation looms on the near horizon.

Electrical Wiring Types, Sizes, and Installation

Much of what you need to know for electrical repairs and remodeling involves wiring—how to identify it, how to buy it, and how to install it with proper connections. If you're planning any electrical project, learning the basics of wiring materials and installation is the best place to start. Understanding basic wiring terminology and identifying the most common types of wire and cable will help when investigating wiring problems and when choosing the wiring for new installation and remodeling projects.

Here are all the basic elements you need to understand about electrical wiring.

Understanding Wire Sizing

The proper wire size is critical to any electrical wire installation. Wire sizing indicates the diameter of the metal conductor of the wire and is based on the American Wire Gauge (AWG) system. The gauge of a wire relates to the wire's current-carrying capacity, or how much amperage the wire can safely handle. When choosing the right size of the wire, you must consider the gauge of the wire, the wire capacity, and what the wire will be used for.

Wires that are not properly matched to the amperage of the circuits they serve can create a notable risk of short circuit and fire.

Non-Metallic (NM) Sheathed Cable

Most interior wiring is done with non-metallic, or NM, cable—also known by the popular brand name "Romex." NM cable is made of three or more wires wrapped inside a flexible plastic jacket, or sheathing. It is used for most interior circuits, such as those for outlets, switches, light fixtures, and appliances. Learn the basics of NM cable to choose the right type for your next electrical project.

Electrical Wire Color Coding

Color coding is used both on the outer sheathing of bundled electrical cables and on the individual conduction wires within cables or inside conduit. Understanding this color coding can help you identify what the wiring is used for and helps maintain consistency within an electrical system.

Cable coloring relates to the size of the wires inside the cable and the cable's amperage rating. For example, white-sheathed NM cable is used for 15-amp circuits, while yellow NM cable is rated for 20-amp circuits.

The coloring on individual conducting wires usually does not indicate a size or rating but rather the standard or preferred use of the wire. For example, black and red wires typically are used for current-carrying or "hot" connections, and white wires usually are grounded "neutral" conductors. Green-insulated wires and bare copper wires are used for grounding wires.

Understanding Electrical Wiring Labeling

Electrical wires and cable have markings stamped or printed on their insulation or outer sheathing. These markings provide important information about the wiring and insulation, including the wire size and material, the type of insulation, the number of wires contained (inside a cable), and any special ratings or characteristics of the wire.

While looking at the color of wire or cable will help you narrow down the options at the store, reading and understanding the labels on wiring is the best way to ensure you get the properly rated material for your project.

Direct Burial Cable

Standard electrical cable is designed to be run indoors, where it stays dry and is protected by wall, ceiling, or floor structures. For outdoor projects or when running wiring underground, you must use direct burial cable, which can be installed underground with or without conduit (depending on local building code rules). With direct burial cable, the individual conducting wires are embedded in solid vinyl to fully protect them from moisture.

How to Strip Electrical Wire

Stripping electrical wire involves removing the plastic insulation surrounding the wire's metal core. It's important to do this carefully so there is no damage to the metal. The procedure is simple but requires a special wire stripping tool and an understanding of how to use it. This is a critical skill—and tool—for DIYers to have for any wiring project.

Maximum Number of Wires Allowed in Conduit

When running individual electrical wires inside conduit, there is a limit to how many wires are allowed. The maximum allowable number is known as the "fill capacity," and this depends on several factors, including the size of the conduit, the gauge of the wires, and the conduit material. Metal (EMT), plastic (PVC), and flexible conduit all have different fill capacities, even when they're nominally the same size.

Wiring an Electrical Circuit Breaker Panel

The electrical panel, or service panel, is the power distribution point of a home electrical system. This is where all of the individual circuits of the house get their power and where they are protected by breakers or fuses. Wiring an electrical panel is a job for a licensed electrician, but DIYers should have a basic understanding of how a panel works and the critical role that breakers play in any system.

Electrical Disconnect Switches

An electrical disconnect switch provides a means to shut off the power to a home's electrical system from an outdoor location. It is typically mounted below the electric meter, either on the side of a home or on the utility company's power pole. Not all homes have a dedicated disconnect. They are commonly used when the service panel (which also serves as the main disconnect) is located indoors and therefore is not accessible to emergency responders or utility workers. Like electrical service panels, a disconnect must be installed by a licensed electrician.

Understanding Electrical Wire Labeling

Wiring sold for electrical projects often carries labeling to help you choose the right product for your needs. Letters, numbers, and wording on wiring labels tell you important information, such as the wire material, the size of the wire, and the type of insulation used on the conducting wires. Labels are found on both individual insulated wires and on insulated cable containing bundles of wires. Cables carry labels indicating the cable type or construction as well as the number of wires inside the cable.

Labels on Non-Metallic Cable (Romex)

The most common type of wiring used in homes is non-metallic (NM) cable, commonly called "Romex," after the popular brand name. New NM cable contains two or more insulated conducting wires and usually a bare ground wire. The wires may be wrapped in paper, and all of the wires are encased in a flexible plastic jacket or sheathing.

The labels on the outer sheathing of NM cable indicate the size, or gauge, of the individual conducting wires, the wire material, the number of wires contained inside the cable, the maximum voltage rating, and whether there is a ground wire present. The wire size and number of wires are indicated with numbers. A ground wire is indicated by "G," "w/G," or "with Ground." The wire material is indicated by "CU" for copper and "AL" for aluminum.

Here are some examples of labels on common cable types used in home wiring:

• 14-2G: Cable contains two insulated wires plus a ground wire; the wires are 14-gauge.

• 14-3G: Cable contains three insulated wires plus a ground wire; the wires are 14-gauge.

• 12-2 w/G: Cable contains two insulated wires plus a ground wire; the wires are 12-gauge.

• 12-3 w/G: Cable contains three insulated wires plus a ground wire; the wires are 12-gauge.

• 600 V: Cable is rated for a maximum of 600 volts; this is standard for residential NM cable.

• TYPE NM-B: Non-metallic type-B cable; this is the current standard for residential installations. "NM-B" cable is more heat-resistant than older "NM" cable.

Underground Feeder Cable

Most NM cable is used in "dry," or interior, locations, where the cable is protected inside wall, ceiling, and floor cavities. Underground feeder (UF) cable is a special type of non-metallic cable that is suitable for "wet" locations, or for unprotected locations like direct burial in the ground. UF cable is usually gray (not white, yellow, orange, or black, like standard NM cable); it is labeled "UF-B" and may include "Sunlight Resistant" or similar wording. UF cable uses the same symbols as standard NM cable to indicate the number and gauge of wires.

Labels on Individual Wires

Individual insulated wires are used in home wiring when an installation calls for conduit—a rigid or flexible protective pipe or tubing through which the wires are run. Electricians buy the individual conducting wire by the spool so they can pull different wires from different spools as needed.

The important labeling on individual wires relates to the wire insulation—the plastic coating that covers the metal conducting wire. The most common types of wire used in home wiring include:

• THHN

• THWN

• THW

• XHHN

Here's what the letters on the labels mean:

• T: Thermoplastic insulation, a fire-resistant material

• H: Heat-resistant; able to withstand temperatures up to 167 F.

• HH: Highly heat-resistant; able to withstand temperatures up to 194 F.

• W: "Wet," or approved for damp and wet locations; this wire is also suitable for dry locations

• X: Insulation made of a synthetic polymer that is flame-retardant

• N: Nylon-coated for resistance to oil and gasoline

Labels on Low-Voltage and Thermostat Wires

Low-voltage wiring used around the home includes small non-metallic cable used for thermostats and other control devices and paired insulated wire used for landscape lighting systems. Wire for landscape lights usually is black and has labeling stamped into the wire insulation. Labels typically include:

• **Wire size:** Indicated by a number (such as 12, for 12-gauge) or a number followed by "AWG," for American Wire Gauge.

• **Number of wires:** Usually indicated by the number 2; landscape wiring typically has two insulated wires stuck together (similar to a lamp cord) and contains no ground wire.

• **Properties:** Wording indicating sunlight-resistance or suitability for underground installation.

Thermostat cable is similar to NM cable but contains four or more small insulated wires and no ground wire. The cable may or may not be labeled. Each wire has its own color to help you connect to the appropriate terminal at the thermostat and the equipment it controls. Although color coding is not universal, the lettering on the thermostat terminals is relatively standard:

- C: Common wire; allows for continuous power flow from the R wire; not all thermostats use this terminal
- R: 24-volt power supply from the furnace transformer
- Rc: Calls for heat or cooling; there may be more than one Rc terminal
- G: Fan
- W: Heat
- Y: Air conditioner

Electrical Wiring Color Coding System

Opening up an outlet or light switch box, you might be confronted with a bewildering array of wires of different colors. Black, white, bare copper, and other colors closely intermingle, yet each one has a specific purpose. Knowing the purpose of each wire will keep you safe and your house's electrical system in top working order.

Electrical Cable and Wire Color Markings

Non-metallic (or NM) 120-volt and 240-volt electrical cable come in two main parts: the outer plastic sheathing (or jacket) and the inner, color-coded wires. The sheathing binds the inner wires together, and its outer markings indicate the number of wires and size of wire (gauge) within the sheathing. The color of the sheathing indicates recommended usages. For example, white sheathing means that the inner wires are 14-gauge and yellow sheathing indicates that they are 12-gauge.

But looking deeper, the color of the wires inside of the sheathing reveals that different colored wires serve different purposes. The National Electrical Code (NEC)says that white or gray must be used for neutral conductors and that bare copper or green wires must be used as ground wires. Beyond that are general, industry-accepted rules about wire color that indicate their purpose.

Black Wires: Hot

Black insulation is always used for hot wires and is common in most standard household circuits.

The term "hot" is used for source wires that carry power from the electric service panel to a destination, such as a light or an outlet. Even though you are permitted to use a white wire as a hot wire by marking it with electrical tape, the opposite is not recommended or allowed. In other words, do not use a black wire as a neutral or ground wire, or for any purpose other than for carrying live electrical loads.

Red Wires: Hot

Red wires are used to designate hot wires.

Red wires are sometimes used as the second hot wire in 240-volt installations. Another useful application for red wires is to interconnect hardwired smoke detectors so that if one alarm is triggered all of the others go off simultaneously.

White Wires With Black or Red Tape: Hot

When a white wire is augmented with a red or black color marking, this often indicates that it is being used as a hot wire rather than a neutral wire. Typically, this is indicated with a band of black or red electrical tape (but other colors may be used) wrapped around the wire's insulation.

For instance, a white wire in a two-wire cable may be used for the second hot wire on a 240-volt appliance or outlet circuit. This white wire should be looped several times around with black electrical tape to show that it is being used for something other than a neutral.

Bare Copper Wires: Ground

Bare copper wires are the most common type of wire used for grounding.

All electrical devices must be grounded. In the event of a fault, grounding provides a safe pathway for electricity to travel. The current passes back to the ground or earth. Bare copper wires connect to electrical devices, such as switches, outlets, and fixtures, as well as metal appliance frames or housings. Metal electrical boxes also need ground connection because they are made of a conductive material. Plastic boxes are nonconductive and do not need to be grounded.

Green Wires: Ground

Green insulated wires are sometimes used for grounding.

Ground screws on electrical devices are often painted green, too. Never use a green wire for any purpose other than for grounding.

White or Gray Wires: Neutral

White or gray indicates a neutral wire.

When examining a white or gray wire, make certain that it has not been wrapped in electrical tape. This would indicate a hot wire. Older wires sometimes may lose their electrical tape wrapping. So, if the box has a loose loop of tape inside of it, there is the possibility that it may have come off of the neutral wire.

The term neutral can be dangerously deceiving as it appears to imply a non-electrified wire. It is important to note that neutral wires may also be carrying power and can shock you. While wires designated as hot (black or red insulated wires) carry power from the service panel (breaker box) to the device, neutral wires carry power back to the service panel. Thus, both hot and neutral wires have the potential to shock and injure you.

Blue and Yellow Wires

Blue and yellow wires are sometimes used as hot wires inside an electrical conduit.

Rarely are blue and yellow wires found in NM cable. Blue wires are commonly used for travelers in a three-way and four-way switch applications.

How an Electrical System Works

Everyone uses electricity in their homes every day, but how does it get there and how is it distributed throughout the home? For electricity to function properly, it must always complete a circuit.

Electricity flows in from one of two 120-volt wires and backs out through a grounded neutral wire. Any flaw in the wire to and from these points will interrupt the current's path and cause a fault in one of your circuits.

Knowing how the power flows into your home, how it's connected, and how it is distributed can help you isolate any problems that occur.

Service Entrance

The utility company's overhead service lines feed the transformer to step down the voltage to feed your home. It then travels to the weather head (service head) which is attached to a conduit connected to a meter box. This assembly is attached with anchor bolts and straps to support the weight of the pipe and wire.

Two 120-volt wires and a grounded neutral wire feed the meter through the weather head. The utility company is responsible for power to the meter, and the homeowner takes it from there.

The service from the utility company to the meter is always live unless it comes and turns it off. If there appears to be a problem on their side of the meter, don't hesitate to call the company to repair the problem. It has special equipment for just such repairs. Never attempt to work on their side of the meter, ever!

Electric Meter

The electric meter is attached to the service entrance pipe and is usually to the side of your house. It may be attached to the utility company's power pole also. It can be fed overhead or underground.

The meter is a watt measuring device supplied by the utility company to track each month's power consumption. There are meters with numbered dials such as a watch on older models and new state-of-the-art digital meters that can be read right from the utility company's office.

Weatherproof Disconnect

In most cases, the utility company will require a weatherproof disconnect right after the meter connection. This is often referred to as a safety switch or service disconnect. This allows the homeowner to disconnect the power from the utility company from the outside of the house without having to get to the electrical panel.

A great reason for this would be a house fire. The fire department can kill the power from outside the home without entering the home. This allows them to spray water on fire without worrying about being electrocuted.

Electrical Panel

Known as the electrical panel, breaker box, fuse box, or service panel, this piece of equipment is the next device in line. This panel's job is to distribute power throughout your home and disconnect power from the incoming feed.

The power comes into the main breaker and is usually 100 or 200 amps. Individual breakers then distribute individual circuits (called branch circuits) throughout your home.

These breakers range in size from 15 to 100 amps. Lighting circuits would be 15 amps, outlet circuits would be 20 amps, and a sub-panel circuit to a garage or tool shed would usually be 60 or 100 amps.

Grounding Wire and Water Ground Connection

The service must be connected to a ground rod outside the house and also bonded around the water meter in the house. A jumper connected on both sides of the meter must be made to allow the meter to be removed without losing a ground connection.

Approved Electrical Boxes

The branch circuits are run into electrical boxes that are mounted inside of the walls of every room of your house. The National Electric Code requires that wires be spliced into boxes.

The reason is to make every connection accessible. For instance, if you splice the wires together and tape them within the wall cavities with no box and cover it with drywall, how will you get back to it to work on the splice if there's a problem? You can open a box at any time.

Switches

Switches come in many different styles. There are single-pole, three-way, four-way, dimmer, and motion-sensing switches. Their purpose is to turn on and off a circuit from different places in your home. Switches are used to control lighting, ceiling fans, receptacles, and appliances. Switches have different amperage ratings depending on the load requirements.

Receptacles

Receptacles, commonly referred to as outlets, are used to provide individual plug-in points for power distribution. The housing market most frequently uses 125-volt as well as 15- and 20-amp receptacles for general household equipment. For appliances such as 250-volt window air-conditioning units, a 250-volt 30-amp outlet is required.

Hopefully, having learned the basic parts of the electrical system will be useful to you in the future. Knowing how everything flows from start to finish helps in tracking down electrical problems that might arise.

CHAPTER TWO

Home Electrical Wiring & Connections

It's time to tackle some wiring projects in your home, but where do you begin? It's important that you know what you're dealing with before you start, so a little lesson in 'Wiring 101' is in order. From understanding the different types of wires you'll find to installing switches, outlets, and a few major appliances, let's look at the basics of home wiring.

The Common Wires in Your Home

Before you begin your first DIY electrical project, you should learn a little about the wires you'll be working with. Wires vary greatly and each is designed for a purpose.

The wiring in your home is chosen to accommodate the load it must carry as well as the conditions it will be exposed to. Some are designed for indoor use while others can be buried. Some are for your panel while others hook up your lights and outlets.

It may be confusing at first, but you will probably deal with only a few types of wire in your home.

Understand Colors and Labeling

Electrical wire has very convenient ways of telling you what it is. Most of the coding is standard, so with a little study, you'll be able to figure out what you have to work with.

Wiring does not come in a variety of colors to make it look good. No, there is a wire color coding system that applies to most wires in your home. Most importantly, you need to know that the black, red, blue, and yellow wires are hot and green is often the ground.

If you look, you will also find a series of letters on a wire. These labels are also standard and will tell you more information about the makeup of the wire. For instance, the code may tell you whether it's aluminum or copper or whether or not it is heat resistant.

As you learn more about wiring, you'll realize just how often you need to know these things.

Wire Size Matters

It is critical in any wiring project that you match the gauge of the wire with the amperage rating of the circuit. Failing to do so can lead to a fire.

A wire's gauge is the physical size of the wire, but the scale is opposite of the wire's circumference. This means that a 2-gauge wire is actually larger than a 14-gauge wire. The size determines how much current can pass through, so the larger wires will be used for your heavier loads.

Installing an Outlet

Many homeowners want to take care of the basic wiring needs for their house. Among the most common projects is installing an outlet. It's a basic project that almost anyone can do if they take the time to understand the process.

You may also want to understand how to wire a split outlet. This comes in handy if, for instance, you want to plug a lamp into an outlet and be able to turn it on from a wall switch.

Simple Installation of a Single-Pole Switch

Light switches are the other electrical installations you might want to handle yourself. The majority of these in homes are what is known as a 'single-pole switch.' They're just as easy to replace as an outlet. Somewhere in your home, you may come across an odd looking switch that makes you stop and wonder. It's likely that this is a three-way switch. They're a little more complicated and used when multiple switches control a single light.

When You Need to Install an Electrical Panel

The majority of homeowners will not mess around with the electric meter or service disconnect and leave these up to the utility company or hire an electrician. However, you might work with the electrical panel.

Whether you're installing a new panel or making repairs on an old one, it's important that you get it right. After all, this is the hub for your entire home's electricity.

Be sure to properly label any connections you make and update them with any changes. Accidentally turning off the lights on your wife in the bathroom when you meant to disconnect the kitchen may lead to some choice words.

Installing a Dishwasher

New appliances come with their own electrical challenges, which is why many people choose to pay for the installation. If you're a true DIY-er, you can install a dishwasher without problems.

The dishwasher comes with two hook-up challenges: the wiring and the water and drain lines. That's why it's a good idea to choose a location near your sink. It will save you time and money.

DIY Wiring for Your Oven

Your electric range may also require your electric prowess. You might find yourself replacing the oven bake element, which is a relatively simple project.

You may also need to connect the cord. The exact method you need to follow is going to depend on whether you have a 3- or 4-prong cord.

Keep in mind that these large appliances carry heavy voltages, so read up on the safety tips. For instance, plugging a loose cord into a receptacle to check the fit can give you a deadly shock.

Don't do it.

Installing Dryer Cords

Why oh why do you have to buy a dryer cord separately? It's one of the great mysteries of home improvement, but it's a fact of life. Next time you need to install that new dryer, you'll be prepared after this tutorial.

Home Electrical Basics

People depend on electricity constantly, and when the power goes out in a storm or there's a tripped breaker or another problem in an electrical circuit, understanding the basic components of an electrical system can help you get things running again. It's also important to know who is responsible for what portion of your electrical service. The utility company handles the line portion of your service, which includes everything up to the attachment point on your house. From there, it's called the load side, and everything on the load side is your responsibility.

Electrical Service Connection and Meter

Your home's electricity starts with the power service and electric meter. The utility company's service cables (whether overhead or underground) extend to your house and connect to the utility's electric meter. The meter measures the amount of electricity your home uses and is the basis for the charges on your electric bill. The meter runs only when electricity is used in the house.

Disconnect Switch

Many home electrical systems include a dedicated disconnect switch that is mounted on an outside wall of the home near the electric meter. In the event of a fire or flash flood, or if work needs to be done on the system, a disconnect switch allows you to shut off the power from outside the home so you don't have to enter the home to turn off the power. If an electrical system does not include a separate disconnect switch, the main circuit breaker in the home's main service panel (breaker box) serves as the system disconnect.

Main Service Panel

After passing through the meter, your electrical service feeds into your home's main service panel, commonly known as the breaker box. Two large "hot" wires connect to big screw terminals, called lugs, inside the service panel, providing all the power to the panel. A third service cable, the neutral, connects to the neutral bus bar inside the panel. In simple terms, electricity is supplied to the house on the hot wires. After it flows through the household system, it is fed back to the utility on the neutral wire, completing the electrical circuit.

Main Circuit Breaker

The service panel contains a large main breaker that is the switch controlling the power to the rest of the circuit breakers inside the panel. It is sized according to your home's service capacity. A standard panel today provides 200-amp (ampere) service. Older panels were sized for 150, 100, or fewer amps (amperes).

A main breaker of 200 amps will allow a maximum of 200 amps to flow through it without tripping. In a tripped state, no current will flow to the panel. In systems without an external disconnect switch, the main breaker serves as the household disconnect.

Turning off the main breaker stops the flow of power to all of the branch circuit breakers in the panel, and therefore to all of the circuits in the house. However, power is always flowing into the panel and to the service lugs even when the main breaker is shut off unless the power is shut off at a separate disconnect switch. Power is always present in the utility service lines and the electric meter unless it is shut off by the utility.

Branch Circuit Breakers

The breakers for the branch circuits fill the panel (usually below) the main breaker. Each of these breakers is a switch that controls the flow of electricity to a branch circuit in the house. Turning off a breaker shuts off the power to all of the devices and appliances on that circuit. If a circuit has a problem, such as an overload or a fault, the breaker automatically trips itself off.

The most common cause of a tripped breaker is a circuit overload. If you're running a high-demand appliance, such as a vacuum, toaster, or heater, and the power goes out, you've probably overloaded the circuit. Move the appliance to a different circuit and reset the breaker by switching it to the ON position. If the breaker trips again—without the appliance plugged in—you must call an electrician. There may be a dangerous fault situation in the circuit.

Devices

Devices are all the things in the house that use electricity, including switches, receptacles (outlets), light fixtures, and appliances. Devices are connected to the individual branch circuits that start at the breakers in the main service panel.

A single circuit may contain multiple switches, receptacles, fixtures, and other devices, or it may serve only a single appliance or receptacle. The latter is called a dedicated circuit. These are used for critical-use appliances, such as refrigerators, furnaces, and water heaters. Other appliances, such as dishwashers and microwaves, usually are on dedicated circuits, too, so that they can be shut off at the service panel without interrupting service to other devices. This also reduces the incidence of overloaded circuits.

Switches

Switches are the devices that turn on and off lights and fans in your home. They come in many different styles and colors to suit your design needs. There are single-pole, three-way, four-way, and dimmer switches. When you flip a switch off, it "opens" the circuit, meaning the circuit is broken or not complete and the power is interrupted. When the switch is on, the circuit is "closed," and power flows beyond the switch to the light or another device it is controlling.

Outlets

Electrical outlets, technically called receptacles, provide power to plug-in devices and appliances. Televisions, lights, computers, freezers, vacuums, and toasters are all good examples of devices that can be plugged into an outlet. Standard outlets in a home are either 15-amp or 20-amp; 20-amp outlets can provide more electricity without tripping a breaker. Special outlets for high-demand appliances, such as electric ranges and clothes dryers, may provide 30 to 50 or more amps of power.

In potentially wet areas of a home, such as bathrooms, kitchens, and laundry rooms, some or all of the outlets must have GFCI (ground-fault circuit-interrupter) protection, provided by GFCI outlets or a GFCI breaker.

Wiring

Your home's wiring consists of a few different types of wiring, including non-metallic cable (commonly called Romex), Bx cable, and wiring concealed in conduit. NM cable is the most common type of circuit wiring. It is suitable for use in dry, protected areas (inside stud walls, on the sides of joists, etc.) that are not subject to mechanical damage or excessive heat.

Bx cable, also known as armored cable, consists of wires running inside a flexible aluminum or steel sheath that is somewhat resistant to damage. It is commonly used where wiring for appliances, such as dishwashers and garbage disposers, is exposed.

Conduit is a rigid metal or plastic tubing that protects individual insulated wires. It is used in garages, sheds, and outdoor applications where the wiring must be protected from exposure.

Wires running inside NM cable, Bx cable, or conduit are sized according to each circuit's amperage. Wire size is given in its gauge number. The lower the gauge, the larger the wire, and the more current it can handle. For example, wiring for 20-amp circuits is 12-gauge, which is heavier than the 14-gauge wiring used for 15-amp circuits.

Indoor and Outdoor Electrical Wiring Safety Codes

Electrical codes are in place to protect you, the homeowner. These general guidelines apply to new installations and will give you the basics of what electrical inspectors are looking for. Be sure to check with your local electrical inspector because local codes may vary from the list provided. In the case of existing housing, the codes will apply if you are updating a home, and it requires an electrical update. It is also suggested that you update if the wiring in your home is unsafe and a danger to your family.

The National Electrical Code has some very specific rules and regulations about underground wiring methods and points of attachment. This is a look at the highlights of the outdoor sections of the code. Electrical wiring is often subjected to wet conditions and all of the elements that Mother Nature can throw at them. Electrical safety around swimming pools, hot tubs, and spas should be of extreme importance to the homeowner.

The NEC and Inspections

The National Electrical Code (NEC) was written to provide a set of rules and regulations to keep the use of electricity in your home safe. Here are the top bathrooms' codes you need to live by to remain safe and keep your electrical devices working properly.

You may wonder why the electrical inspector seems to be so tough on you when he explains all of the requirements in your bathroom. You may ask why you need things like GFCi's and exhaust fans. He may tell you that you need a separate circuit for your outlet, but after you consider everything that will probably be plugged into it, you soon see that the inspector is there to help you to have an effective and safe electrical plan.

Bathroom Electrical Codes

Each bathroom should have a circuit for lighting and an exhaust fan. This may include a blower-heater-light combination.

There should also be a 20-amp circuit, separate from the lighting circuit, to provide power for an outlet to feed things like curling irons, razors, hair dryers, and even portable milk house heaters.

Connected to the outlet circuit, you should install a ground fault circuit interrupter (GFCI) to protect the user. A GFCI trips and disconnects the circuit power if it senses a difference in potential on the circuit, like a short circuit or a path to ground, which could be right through your body. This device is very important and can save your life!

Since bathrooms are wet, switches should be grounded as well to give any stray voltage a direct path to ground, instead of through you. You'd hate to get out of the shower, soaking wet, and get shocked by touching a switch.

Install at least one ceiling-mounted light fixture to allow ample lighting. This may be in addition to wall sconces or strip lighting in the bathroom.

Place exhaust fans or heater-fan-light combinations far enough from the bathtub, shower, or hot tub so that no one can stand in water and touch it.

Just remember, these are the bare minimum requirement, and you can add more circuits as you see fit to accommodate the load of the appliance you plan to plug in or add to your bathroom.

Kitchen

A kitchen should have a separate circuit for each appliance with a motor. The microwave, refrigerator, garbage disposal, and dishwasher would be the major appliances included. Generally, the code requires that you install a minimum of two receptacle circuits in the area above the countertop. An electric range, cooktop, or oven must be wired to a dedicated 240-volt circuit.

Living Room, Dining Room, and Bed Rooms

These rooms require that a wall switch is placed beside the entry door of the room so that you can light the room before entering it. It can either control a ceiling light, a wall light, or an outlet connected to a desk lamp. The ceiling fixture must be controlled by a wall switch and not a pull chain type light. Wall receptacles should be placed no farther than 12 feet apart. Dining rooms usually require a separate 20-amp circuit for one outlet used for a microwave, entertainment center, or window air conditioner.

Stairways

Special care is needed in stairways to ensure all of the steps are lighted properly. Three-way switches are required at the top and bottom of the stairs. If the stairs turn, you may need to add additional lighting to accommodate the area to be lit.

Hallways

These areas can be long and need adequate lighting. Be sure to place enough lighting so shadows are not cast when walking. Remember, hallways are often escape routes in the event of inclement weather and emergencies. A hallway over 10 feet long is required to have an outlet for general purpose. Three-way switches are required for the two ends of the hallway. If there are more doors throughout the hallway, say a bedroom or two, then you may want to add addition four-way switches to the circuit outside the door of each room.

Closets

Closets must have one globe covered fixture controlled by a wall switch. Exposed bulb fixtures, like pull-chain fixtures, get hot and come in contact with clothing or other combustible materials stored in closets. Although your existing home may have these fixtures, it is recommended that you change them for safety reasons.

Laundry Room

The washer and dryer should have its own 20-amp receptacle. In the case of an electric dryer, a separate 240-volt circuit should be installed.

Attached Garage

Inside the garage, there should be at least one switch controlling the lighting. It is recommended that three-way switches be installed for convenience between the doors. This lighting should be in addition to any garage door lighting that you may have. Garages need a separate circuit for at least one outlet. This is generally required to be a GFCI outlet. You should check your local code to be sure. When in doubt, make it a GFCI. Any outside outlets connected must be either a GFCI outlet or an outlet connected to a GFCI breaker.

Remember that the electrical codes are in place for your safety. Although you may believe that they are overkill at times, these practices save lives every day. When it comes to electrical safety, don't become a statistic! Follow the rules of the codes and be sure to have your local electrical inspector give you the green light for the safety of your family's sake.

Checking for Incorrect Electrical Wiring

By identifying electrical wiring hazards before problems appear, you can make your home safer and possibly prevent a fire or a dangerous electrical shock. Even the humble electrical outlet or light switch can have numerous things that can go wrong, most of them resulting from faulty installation. Here, then, is a list of wiring problems you might encounter by simply peering into an outlet or switch box with a flashlight. Many of these are easy to fix, but if you find a lot of them, you might want to call in an electrician for an expert inspection of your entire electrical system.

Safety First... Turn off the Power

Before working on any electrical circuit or device, always turn off the power to the entire circuit by switching off the appropriate breaker in your home's service panel (breaker box).

After you've switched off the breaker, test any circuit wires or devices you'll be inspecting with a non-contact voltage tester. This inexpensive tool is about the size and shape of a permanent marker and allows you to test for power without touching any wires. Simply touch the tip of the tester to the wire in question (or insert the tip into an outlet slot or touch it to any device terminal). The tester can detect voltage through the wiring insulation, so you don't have to find the bare end of the wire, as you do with some other testers. If there's voltage, the tester lights up.

No light, no voltage.

Reversed Connections

Most electrical outlets (properly called receptacles) today are grounded three-prong outlets. They have one long straight slot, one short straight slot and a roundish ground slot to accept the three prongs of a grounded plug. Older, ungrounded, outlets have only two straight slots, one long and one short. That's why you often have to flip over a plug to fit it into an outlet; it goes in only one way. This long/short design is called polarized and is a safety feature that predates the standard grounded outlet.

Polarized outlets and plugs ensure that electricity flows in one direction only. This makes things like lamps and many appliances more safe to operate. But here's the catch: If you connect the circuit wires to the wrong terminals on an outlet, the outlet will still work but the polarity will be backward. When this happens, a lamp, for example, will have its bulb socket sleeve energized rather than the little tab inside the socket. Guess which you're more likely to touch? You want the tab energized, not the sleeve.

Inside an outlet's electrical box, the black (hot) wire should be connected to the brass-colored terminal on the outlet. The white (neutral) wire should be connected to the silver-colored terminal. If these connections are backward, the polarity is wrong.

Proper Grounding

In a modern home, almost every part of the electrical system is grounded, meaning it has an unbroken (if usually not direct) connection to the earth outside the house. When something goes wrong, such as a short or fault, electricity flows safely to the earth via the grounding system.

Homes that date back to the 1950s and earlier may have few or no true ground connections. Is this dangerous? It can be. Sometimes very dangerous. But the fact is, most of these homes operate just fine without grounded circuits. That said, if you're adding new circuits or updating any part of an electrical system, you should always include a ground. It's not just smart; it's the law.

If you have outlets on ungrounded circuits you can replace them with GFCIs, or ground-fault circuit-interrupters. These are special outlets that shut off the power if they detect a dangerous ground fault, helping to protect you against shock. They do NOT provide a ground, but they do make using the outlet a lot safer.

One simple way to test outlets for grounding is to plug in a receptacle tester. If the tester indicates an "open ground," the outlet may have no means of grounding or there may be a ground wire but it's improperly connected. It also could be grounded to a metal electrical box but the box is not properly grounded.

Too Many Wires Under Terminals

Installing more than one wire under any standard screw terminal is not only a stupid move, it's a lazy one at that. It is nearly impossible to properly tighten two wires under a single terminal. This usually results in a loose connection. And loose wires are a very bad thing. If you find more than one wire connected to an outlet or switch, correct the problem by joining the wires with a wire connector and include a pigtail, a short length of the same type of wire. Connect the pigtail--and only the pigtail--to the screw terminal in question.

Proper Amount of Wire Insulation

Although it may not seem important, proper insulation length is very important on wire connection points. Stripping a wire to the proper length makes for a great connection. Stripping too much insulation exposes the bare wire too much and can become a point where someone can touch the wire or the bare wire may come in contact with the box or another wire, like the ground wire. in this case, some folks just cover the exposed wires with electrical tape, but the proper method is to re-strip the wire end to proper length.

Too little wire shouldn't be a problem then, right? Wrong! Too little insulation means that some or all of the terminal is in contact with the insulation and not the bare wire. This either means that there is a limited connection, with resistance due to the insulation, or no connection at all.

When stripping wire for a screw terminal, remove about 3/4 inch of insulation from the wire end. Shape the bare wire end into a hook and attach it to the terminal so the open end of the hook is on the right;

this means the hook tightens around the screw as the screw is turned. When the connection is complete, the wire insulation should almost touch the screw, but none of it should be under the screw.

Common Wire Connection Problems and Their Solutions

A great many electrical problems around the house are traced to different versions of the same essential problem: wire connections that are made improperly or that have loosened over time. You may have inherited the problem from a previous owner or from an electrician who did an inadequate job, or perhaps it's the result of work you did yourself. Many wire connection problems are no one's fault but are simply the result of time. Wires are under a constant cycle of heating and cooling, expansion and contraction. Every time a switch is used or appliances are plugged in, and the natural result of all this usage is that wire connections can loosen over time.

Your electrical system has a lot of safeguards against danger from bad wire connections, such as its grounding system, its circuit breakers, and GFCI and AFCI protection. Still, there is danger from sparking and arcing whenever there is a loose wire connection in your system. Many of these problems are quite easy for a homeowner to spot and repair, while others are best handled by a professional electrician. Understanding where these problems commonly occur will help you decide how to handle them.

Tools and Materials

• Flashlight

• Wire strippers

• Screwdrivers

• Utility knife

• Wire connectors (wire nuts)

• Eye protection

• Electrical wire in various gauges

Here are six very common places that wire connection problems occur.

Loose Wire Connections at Switches and Outlets

By far the most common problem is when screw terminal connections at wall switches and outlets become loose. Because these fixtures get the most use within an electrical system, these are the places to look first if you suspect wire connection problems. Loose wire connections at a switch, outlet, or light fixture are often signaled by a buzzing or crackling sound or by a light fixture that flickers.

To address this problem, it involves first turning off the power to the suspected wall switch, light fixture, or outlet. With the power shut off, you can remove the cover plate and use a flashlight to carefully examine the screw terminals inside where the wires are connected. If you find any that are loose, carefully tighten the screw terminals down onto the wires. In all likelihood, this will fix the problem.

Sometimes, you may find that the wire connections are made via push-in fittings on the back of the switch or outlet. This method of connection is notorious for being prone to failure—so much so that most professional electricians don't use the push-in fittings at all, but instead make all wire connections with the screw terminal connections on the sides of the switch or outlet. If you find that your device is made with the push-in fittings, you might want to remove them and reconnect the wires to the screw terminals on the device.

Finally, if there are pass-through wire connections inside the box that are made with wire nuts or another type of connector, check these to make sure the wires are tightly joined together. A loose connector is also a common source of problems.

Wire Connections Made With Electrical Tape

A classic wire connection error is when wires are joined together with electrical tape rather than a wire nut or other sanctioned connector.

To fix the problem, first, turn off the power to the circuit. Then, remove the electrical tape from the wires and clean them. Make sure there is the proper amount of exposed wire showing (for most connectors, this means about 3/4 inch), then join the wires together with a wire nut or other approved connector (there are now push-in connectors that some pros like to use).

If the wire ends are damaged, you can cut off the ends of the wires and strip off about 3/4 inch of insulation to make a proper wire nut connection.

Two or More Wires Under One Screw Terminal

Another common wire connection problem is when you find two or more wires held under a single screw terminal on a switch or outlet. This is a clear sign of amateur work and a distinct fire hazard. It is allowable to have a single wire under each of the two screw terminals on the side of an outlet or switch, but it is a code violation to have two wires wedged under a single screw. This is most often seen when two bare copper grounding wires are found under the grounding screw on the outlet or switch, but you also may occasionally find hot wires or neutral wires connected to a single screw terminal.

To fix this problem, once again, this repair involves first shutting off the power. Then, the two offending wires are removed from their screw terminal. Cut a 6-inch pigtail wire of the same color as the two wires (use a green pigtail if you are joining two bare copper grounding wires). Strip 3/4 inch of insulation from each end of the pigtail, then join one end to the two wires you just disconnected, using a wire connector (wire nut). Now, attach the free end of the pigtail wire to the screw terminal that once held the two wires.

You have essentially created a bridge, or pathway, that connects both wires to the desired screw terminal on the outlet or switch.

Note: Make sure the pigtail wire is the same wire gauge as the circuit wires. A 15-amp circuit normally uses 14-gauge wire; a 20-amp circuit uses 12-gauge wire.

Exposed Wires

It is quite common, especially with amateur electrical work, to see a screw terminal connection or wire nut connection where it has too much (or too little) exposed copper wire showing at the wires. With screw terminal connections, there should be enough bare copper wire stripped to wrap entirely around the screw terminal but not so much that excess bare copper wire extends out from the screw. The excess exposed wire can short out if it touches a metal box or other wires. Wires should be wrapped clockwise around the screw terminals; if they are reversed, they can be prone to loosening.

With wire nut connections, all of the bare copper wire should be hidden under the plastic cap, with no exposed wire showing at the bottom of the wire nut. To fix the problem, turn off the power to the device, then disconnect the wires and either clip off the excess wire or strip off additional insulation so the proper amount of wire is exposed. Then, reconnect the wires to their screw terminal or wire nut. Tug lightly on the wires to make sure they are securely connected.

Loose Connections on Circuit Breaker Terminals

A less common problem is when the hot wires on circuit breakers in the main service panel are not tightly connected to the breaker. When this happens, you may notice lights flickering or service problems on fixtures all along the circuit. When making connections to circuit breakers, be sure to strip the proper amount of wire insulation from the wire and make sure that only the bare wire is placed under the terminal slot before tightening. Insulation under the connection slot is a code violation.

To fix the problem, repairs at the main service panel should be handled by a professional electrician. Amateurs should attempt these repairs only if they are quite experienced and knowledgeable about electrical systems.

The electrician will address this problem by turning off the breaker then unclipping it from the hot bus bar in the main service panel. He or she will check the hot wire connected to the breaker to make sure that the screw is tight and that there is no insulation under the terminal and no excess bare copper wire exposed. With repair complete, the electrician will snap the breaker back into place on the hot bus bar and turn the breaker back on.

Faulty Neutral Wire Connections at Circuit Breaker Panels

Another less common problem—and another that is usually handled by a pro—is when the white circuit wire is not correctly mounted to the neutral bus bar in the main service panel. Symptoms here will be similar to those with a faulty hot wire.

To fix this problem, the electrician will check to make sure the neutral wire is sufficiently stripped and correctly attached to the neutral bus bar.

CONCLUSION

Residential electrical wiring systems start with the utility's power lines and equipment that provide power to the home, known collectively as the service entrance. The power is run through an electric meter, which records how much energy is used in the home and is the basis for the monthly electric bill. In general, the utility company's jurisdiction stops with the meter. After that point, all of the electrical equipment is the homeowner's responsibility.

The service entrance is the equipment that brings electrical power to the home. Most residential service includes three wires: two cables carrying 120 volts each (for a total of 240 volts) and one grounded neutral wire. If the cables are hung overhead, they are collectively called a service drop. If they are routed underground, they are known as a service lateral. A service drop connects to the home at a service head, or weather head, on the roof or exterior wall of the house.

Once the power reaches the house via the service drop or service lateral cables, it passes through the electric meter, which may be mounted on an exterior wall or may be located inside the home's breaker box. The meter records all electricity used by the home, measured in kilowatt-hours, or kWh. A 100-watt light bulb burning for 10 hours uses 1 kWh of electricity. Meters may be analog or digital type, although most new meters are digital and can be read remotely by the utility company.

The main service panel, commonly known as the breaker box or circuit breaker panel, distributes power to all circuits throughout the building. Each circuit has a breaker that can shut itself off in the event of a short circuit or overload to cut power to the circuit. Old homes may have fuses instead of breakers. Fuses are just as effective as breakers, but most new panels today use breakers instead of fuses. It is important to note that power coming from the service lines to the electric meter, and then to the main service panel, is always live. Before working on these areas the power company must shut off the power. The power going out of the panel to the household circuits can be shut off by the main breaker in the service panel, but the power coming into the panel is not affected by the main breaker.

www.ingramcontent.com/pod-product-compliance
Lightning Source LLC
Chambersburg PA
CBHW072007170726
47999CB00013B/988